The Most Important Day of Your Life: Are You Ready?

Maria Dancing Heart Hoaglund

Infinite Hope & Healing, Dancing

Bridge to Dreams Publishing, Lynnwood, Washington

ISBN: 978-0-9752932-1-8
Library of Congress Control Number: 2010903163

Published by Bridge to Dreams Publishing,
13619 Mukilteo Spwy., D5-411; Lynnwood, WA 98087

Printed by Snohomish Publishing Co., Inc., Snohomish, WA USA
Cover and book design: Snohomish Publishing Co., Inc.
Earth Angel cover art by Josephine Wall

Editor: Barbara J. Fandrich

This book was published in a grassroots fashion. The author maintained full control of the content in order to protect the integrity and layout of the material. None of the information herein is intended to replace any medical or spiritual care or relationships with health care or spiritual care professionals. Rather, the aim is to enhance and complement those relationships and communication, allowing everyone to explore more deeply and fully.

www.changewithcourage.com

www.soulbaskets.com

To Elizabeth Kubler-Ross

Stephen Levine

and
all the teachers
who have taught us about
the beauty and grace of death
along life's path

May this book further illuminate the way
toward death with increased love, joy, hope and understanding.

Your natural state is that of Foreverness.

— Abraham-Hicks

Funny how you'll plan every aspect of every trip
Except the most important one you'll ever take!

— NHPCO website

Table of Contents

Foreword

In *The Most Important Day of Your Life: Are You Ready?* Maria *Dancing Heart* Hoaglund has created a fine amalgam of stories, guiding images, and soul exercises for those who seek understanding and loving care to overcome our anxiety of death. In my work as an educator, researcher, and clinician, I deepen my learning of the elements of empathic balance. And as a spiritual care responder, my story and the story of the care-seeker are delicately and forever moving within a range of mutual love. This is a constant and ever stirring dance of hearts. And *Dancing Heart* reminds us that such a balancing can be encouraged and sustained through our intentional practice of appreciating and preparing for death – the natural ending of life that we all face.

This work reads tenderly, lovingly, like an interview with a hospice counselor. We are treated to a multi-cultural embrace of our life's most important day by a person whose gentleness and respect for the needs of the care-seeker are also shown toward herself – on her own path to self-love. *Dancing Heart* encourages us to set ourselves free from constipating expectations and traditions; she guides us to prepare for experiencing death with flexibility and honor. *Dancing Heart* has again responded to us by providing a spiritual health resource that serves as a *lifebook for last days* – no matter the number left.

– George Henry Grant,
MDiv, PhD, Emory Center for Pastoral
Services, Emory University

Introduction

Shortly after the first edition of *The Last Adventure of Life* was published, I was in a health food store on Whidbey Island where the book was being sold. A Buddhist gentleman, also a volunteer firefighter I discovered, happened to walk into the store; and we struck up a conversation. At one point in our animated exchange the man exclaimed, "In Buddhism, birth is considered the hard part. Death is easy because we have the whole rest of our lives to prepare for it." I recall thinking to myself: Wow, that's an intriguing perspective on death. I wonder what we Americans could learn from this perspective? How would our lives change in a good way if we could look at our lives as a spiritual practice to prepare for our final graduation from earthly life? In truth, every day of our lives provide us with wonderful opportunities to prepare for the last adventure of life.

Another gem I've learned through the Buddhist perspective is that the actual moment of our death is of great significance. In Buddhist thought, "the moment of death is an exceptionally powerful opportunity for purifying karma." At the actual time of death, there are two things that truly count according to Tibetan Buddhism: Whatever we have done over the course of our lives, and the state of mind that we are in when we are in the process of making the final transition. Even if a person has accumulated a great deal of negative karma over the course of their lives, if that person is able to really make a change of heart at the moment of death, it can influence their future and positively transform their karma. (*The Tibetan Book of Living and Dying*, Sogyal Rinpoche, p. 223)

I invite you to join me through this book on a quest to unearth some of the best kept secrets around death, grief, and hospice. You might learn to go deeper spiritually. You can reflect on how expansive your life is and how lovingly, courageously, and meaningfully you can live it. And who knows? You just might decide – as the Celtic way suggests – to die before you die, so that when you finally let go of your earthly life, there'll be no need to die!

When I was putting *The Last Adventure of Life* together I came across the quote **"Funny how you'll plan every aspect of every trip except the most important one you'll ever take!"** My hope and prayer is that you will find new doorways in this book that will bring you fresh perspectives and tools on how to prepare for your final transition. By the way, it is never too early to start preparing.

Best of all, I hope you may discover new ways to more deeply honor the true gift that the Present Moment is.

1

Life and Death Go Hand in Hand: Bringing Death Back to Life

"Our scientific power has outrun our spiritual power. We have guided missiles, and misguided men."
— *Martin Luther King, Jr.*

Somewhere along the way in American society we lost our way, and life and death became separated. Rabbi Schachter-Shalomi says that it's only during the last one hundred years that death has become "pathologized" because we've taken it to the hospital. This rings true for me because the tendency in our hospitals is to keep people alive literally at all costs; my heart aches for the doctors who feel like failures when a patient dies on one of their shifts.

When I talk with older people, some of them recall the days when the parlor was in the living room. Before and after a person died, they would typically be resting in the parlor and the "wake" would take place there, too – after the individual had died. However, now when we hear the word "parlor" we think of the funeral parlor; the funeral homes have for the most part taken over the process that takes place after a person dies. This need not be so, and there is a movement in our country to begin to bring death and even funerals back into the hands of homes and families. (For more resources on this, see the "Home-based, Natural Funeral Services" section in the last chapter of my first book, *The Last Adventure of Life*, or the Links page at my website: **www.changewithcourage.com**.)

Clarissa Pinkola Estes tells a story that reminds us that death comes perched on our shoulder when we are born into this world. Death lives with us and beside us throughout our lives. However, in our materially oriented culture, we tend to lose sight of this. Even our doctors and healthcare professionals are trained to keep people alive by any means. Consider how much more gracious our lives might be if we could simply invite death back into our lives and into our living rooms, recognizing that every day is precious – life is a true gift – and we never know when we might be called or welcomed back to our true Home on the Other Side.

In the beautiful true story shared in *Molokai* (O. A. Bushnell, 1975) about Father Damien, the priest who went to live with the lepers on the Hawaiian island of Molokai, Fr. Damien shares these words with Caleb, a member of the leper colony:

> "Caleb, Caleb, my son. Do not be so afraid of Death. Look upon Death, so you may know what life is. When you have done this, then you will no longer be afraid. What is there to fear? Death is but another form of the mercy of God. It is the last and the greatest of [God's] gifts. Have you not seen this? Death is not to be feared: it is to be welcomed, when it comes, for it is the messenger of God. And life for us here on earth is but the season of waiting, until God is ready to invite us to the great feast God prepares for us in Heaven." (p. 505)

It is my fervent hope that we will all take the time and effort to dive deeper into our spiritual lives and remember the interconnectedness of life and death. As we come to lessen our fear around death and become more comfortable with the mystery of life itself, we will open up the possibility for a deeper and richer, more meaningful life – as well as a good, well-prepared for death.

> *Fear knocked at the door.*
> *Love answered.*
> *No one was there.*
> *– ancient wisdom*

Suggested Exercise

Practice: I Could Die Today

The following is an exercise I received at a weekend retreat on "Embracing Death as a Spiritual Path," led by Rodney Smith, a teacher of Insight Meditation. I asked him for permission to use this exercise, and he shared that he got it from Wayne Muller, an author I quoted in my first book. (See the end of chapter 5 of *The Last Adventure of Life*, "Don't Ask Why.")

Pick a simple daily activity, something you do at least once every day, such as turning on the faucet, turning on a light switch, getting into or out of your car, putting on or taking off your clothes, climbing a stairway, taking a drink of water, or opening a door.

Choose one of these activities. Then, for one week, whenever you perform this activity, say to yourself: "I could die today."

Stop for just a moment in the process of this activity and reflect on the truth of the simple phrase, "I could die today."

What if this could be true? It is true, you know. Any one of us could die at any time, any day. What if YOU were to die today?

What feelings arise within when you think this thought? Who comes to mind? What activities? What hopes and dreams? What burdens or responsibilities do you feel liberated from?

Pay attention to what arises within when you say this to yourself every day: I could die today.

Note: If the above exercise is too much for you to do, begin simply by writing down some things that scare you about death. Why does death scare you so? Where did you first develop your fear? Was it a particular experience that you had? Or something someone told you? Reflect on death and see what comes up for you.

If you are interested in reading more on the Buddhist perspective on the moment of death, I invite you to read Chapter 14 of *The Tibetan Book of Living and Dying* (pp. 223 – 243).

Finding Humor in Death

How To Get To Heaven From Ireland: This is a joke that a friend received from a British friend.

I was testing the children in me Dublin Sunday school class to see if they understood the concept of getting into heaven. I asked them, "If I sold my house and my car, had a big garage sale and gave all the proceeds to the church, would that get me into heaven?"

"NO!" the children answered.

I continued. "If I cleaned the church every day, mowed the garden, and kept everything tidy, would that get me into heaven?"

Again, the answer was "NO!" By now I was starting to smile.

"Well, then," I asked, "if I was kind to animals and gave sweets to all the children, and loved my husband, would that get me into heaven?"

Again, all the children answered "NO!"

I was fairly bursting with pride for them as I went on: "Then how can I get into heaven?"

A six year-old boy shouted out, "Y'VE GOTTA BE FOOKN' DEAD!"

It's a curious race, the Irish.

2

Hospice Work – Like Having a Near Death Experience in Slow Motion

"Your natural state is that of Foreverness."
– Abraham-Hicks

I remember an interview in which a guest I invited to join the show with me talked about her near death experience (NDE). Diane Goble, a remarkable woman who lived through her own NDE and now serves as a transition guide, spoke about the experience as a tremendous expansion of consciousness. As I look back on my years of work with hospice as a spiritual and bereavement counselor, I see that the entire experience has been not unlike a NDE for me: I did not actually experience my own physical death, but I came so close to so many who were experiencing the dying process and the depths of the grieving process that much of it rubbed off on me. It was as if a part of me was having a taste of part of the experience, too.

In fact, when I first left the parish ministry and began doing the bereavement counseling, then later the spiritual work for hospice, I found myself like a kid in the candy store.

I was so eager to learn more about the mystical aspect of life that I soaked up all the new information I could that was coming at me on a regular basis. Being free of parish work, I also had more time and flexibility than before, not to mention the permission to explore astrology, numerology, and other metaphysical systems of thought. I was somehow instinctively drawn to them.

I remember excitedly heading north to Stanwood one day to receive my first astrological reading. During the reading I recall thinking: Wow, the Universe really knows me – perhaps like no one else understands me. And the astrologer commented that I was using astrology just the way it is meant to be used: I was going through a time of great change and upheaval in my life, and the reading confirmed this. It was as if the Universe was letting me know, reassuring me that "No, you're not going crazy. Rather, you're just where you're supposed to be in your life!" I felt so encouraged by the whole experience.

Around this same time, I was connecting in a deeper way with a great aunt in my life named Great Aunt Gladys. I knew that she was rather unique and special because of something that had happened some years previously. I was serving the Japanese Congregational Church at the time. The ministry had its own challenges, not only because the bilingual, bicultural church had dwindled in its size and I was working with some very difficult personalities, but because I had to prepare a sermon in both English and Japanese every week. Due to my tendency to procrastinate, I would often be working on the Japanese translation of my sermon into the late hours of Saturday evening.

One Saturday night, I was particularly discouraged and staying up quite late to do the translating. Completely out of the blue, I received a phone call from my Aunt Martha, daughter-in-law of Gladys, who called to let me know that Great Aunt

Gladys had a message for me. The message went something like this: "You're going through a pretty rough stretch right now, Martha (my name for the first forty years of my life), but hang in there because better times are ahead." What a fortuitous message to receive on a night like that! I remember wondering how in the world Great Aunt Gladys – or "Nana," as her family liked to call her – had known that I was struggling that night, for I really did not know Gladys very well at the time.

Gradually, over time, I did come to know this woman of part Native American descent, as the powerful intuitive and psychic woman that she was. By the time I began working with hospice, we were getting together from time to time in her apartment to have a bite to eat. In hindsight, these visits with Great Aunt Gladys were invaluable to me as I came to learn a tremendous amount about the metaphysical world that I had never known before. It was as if this unique and deeply spiritual woman of Roman Catholic background gave me the courage and permission I needed to step outside the box of Christianity to see what I could see and hear with new eyes and new ears.

For example, Great Aunt Gladys would share with me mystical stories that had happened to her. She was an unassuming woman, a hospital janitor for a good portion of her life in order to supplement her small family's income. She told me that on occasion she would see a hospital patient nearing the time of their death. On one such occasion, she was privileged to see the "silver cord" that keeps a person attached to their body. Since the person had died, she saw this cord disengage from the person and float away from the dead body. (I have also learned that when we dream, we typically leave our bodies when experiencing our dreams. During our sleep, however, the chord that connects the soul to the body remains attached; thus, we return to our bodies when we awaken.)

Gladys also shared many mystical experiences she had had with the spirits who came to visit her – usually beneficent, but occasionally maleficent, like the one who kept knocking at her from under her bed! I also discovered along the way that Gladys's mother became a Unity minister toward the later years of her life.

I recall going to a workshop once in which we wrote our own spiritual autobiographies. I realized at this workshop that Great Aunt Gladys had played a most significant role in my life as she was the only woman who stood so clearly outside the religious box and was able to give me permission at a critical juncture in my life to explore and learn new things in new ways. As I look back over my life, I am deeply grateful to this humble woman who showed up just when I needed her most.

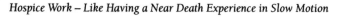

Suggested Exercise

Practice: Write a Brief Spiritual Autobiography

What might your spiritual biography look like? Write down the key persons in your life and a few sentences about their spiritual lives and how they have made a difference in your spiritual life.

Finding Humor in Death

A 54-year-old woman had a heart attack and was taken to the hospital. While on the operating table, she had a near death experience. Seeing God, she asked "Is my time up yet?" God said, "No, you have another 43 years, 2 months, and 8 days to live."

Upon recovery, the woman decided to stay in the hospital and have a face-lift, liposuction, breast implants, and a tummy tuck. She even had someone come in and change her hair color and brighten her teeth!

Since she had so much more time to live, she figured she might as well make the most of it. After her last operation, she was released from the hospital. While crossing the street on her way home, she was killed by an ambulance. Arriving in front of God, she demanded, "I thought you said I had another 43 years? Why didn't you pull me from out of the path of the ambulance?"

God replied, "I didn't recognize you!"

– Author unknown

3

The Simple Power of Being a Loving Witness

"The greatest thing you'll ever learn is just to love and be loved in return."

— Eden Ahbez

I was sharing a quiet conversation with a man stricken with cancer. He was a small, balding man in lounge wear, seated in a comfortable chair in his home. He had a cranky, sometimes even hostile wife who'd been struggling with dementia. Their only son, a policeman I'd met before in his flashy uniform, was doing his best to support his ailing parents.

"Why are you people so nice?" the man asked suddenly. I'm not sure now how I responded, but I know it made me feel grateful about how our hospice team was making a positive impact on this man's life as it was coming to an end.

We Americans tend to focus most of our time on doing things rather than honoring the gift of simply being. At the end of life, however, a person usually has to shift from doing to being as he or she gradually prepares for death. It can be

13

extremely helpful if this person has someone to simply be with them, listen attentively to them, and encourage them along the way. Not only is this a wonderful gift to the dying, but I learned it can also be one of the greatest gifts of a lifetime to be the one who sits with and listens to the person who's preparing to die.

There is a tremendous amount of grief and letting go that needs to be borne as death encroaches. The body is usually growing weaker, so the loss of physical control becomes a big issue. As the body becomes more limited, much grief may need to be expressed, and the simple presence of another human being is so appreciated at this time. I discovered that the question "What will I say?" was not as pertinent as "How much can I take in?" I needed to learn to simply be with and hold space for the suffering and pain, as well as the joy, exuberance, and curiosity that I was witnessing.

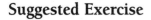

Suggested Exercise

Practice: Being Fully in the Present Moment

Practice simply "being present" to the present moment for twenty to thirty minutes. You could meditate, take a walk, preferably in a beautiful place, or simply stare out the window for a long while. While you are "being," pay attention to your thoughts. Notice how active your mind is and see if you can quiet it down as you take some good, deep breaths. Keep your focus on your breathing, or on a particular word, phrase, or mantra.

Then, notice how you feel afterward. What did you notice during your "being" time? How does it affect how you feel and do things afterward?

Finding Humor in Death

I had just come on duty, was in the middle of getting report about a dying gentleman down the hall; his son was very attentive and was with him all shift. Up to the nurses desk comes the son with a bereaved look on his face to report that his Dad had just passed away. The PM nurse and myself went down the hall with the son and into his dad's room. The son had taken it upon himself to cover his dad's face with the top sheet. I guess he thought that was proper according to the movies, or whatever. As we were bending over the dad getting ready to remove the sheet, the man let out one huge last breath. WHOA!!! I don't know who jumped higher the son, or we two nurses! Well it was the last breath and the dad did pass peacefully. When we two nurses were alone, I admit we just cracked up at our own responses to seeing that sheet puff up over dear Dad's face! NO disrespect meant here.

– Author unknown, found on the Internet

May your body be cold before the devil knows your dead!
– Received through an Irish patient

4

Maintaining Attentive Ears with an Open Heart

"Everyone wants to go to heaven; no one wants to go today!"

In her book *Eat, Pray, Love*, Elizabeth Gilbert shares a fascinating image that she received from an Indonesian medicine man in response to her question: How can I have a lasting experience of God – devote myself to God while also enjoying the delights of the world? In response, the shaman showed her a drawing he had sketched during a meditation. It was a picture of an androgynous human figure, hands clasped in prayer, standing on four legs. Where the head would normally be, the figure had some wild foliage of ferns and flowers, and over the heart area was a smiling face.

The shaman explained that in order to live in the world but not of it, or to know God more fully in daily life, one must be first and foremost well grounded in the world – as if on four feet. Then, one must "let go" of the head and look through the heart. This image has stayed with me as I work to release judgment and my analytical mind and tune more fully into my heart. If I can see the world and all people through the eyes of my heart, then I can be so much more gentle and gracious with everyone and everything! I can tune into the unconditional love that I desire to cultivate in my life, too.

I believe that hospice work has helped me to tune in to my heart more and put my analytical mind into the background. This seemed to happen especially because as I was sitting with people, I found myself being encouraged to listen attentively to the one I happened to be with. Sometimes there were no words, so I needed to pick up on other cues – body language, eye movements, and the like. Sometimes the words spoken were quite unexpected or not my kind of language, so it would stretch my world view. This experience of truly being present with another human being in the fullness of who they were at that moment encouraged me to go deeper and listen harder – pay more attention and speak or "chatter" less.

This reminds me of an experience I had very early on in my seminary training. I was in the midst of a year of Clinical Pastoral Education in Denver. We were doing the work of a chaplain as interns, but also reflecting intensively on our work and learning through didactic sessions. I was covering the cancer ward at the Presbyterian Hospital in town. One day I went in to visit "the Captain," as we called him – a man who'd spent many years directing ships. He was very close to his death from cancer. At some early point in our visit I took his hand, or he took mine, and we made a strong connection.

After a period of time of speaking and praying together, I felt we'd had as much contact as was needed – or comfortable for me, anyway. I began to let "Cap" know that I would be on my way, whereupon Cap quickly let me know that he wanted me to keep holding his hand and stay with him for awhile. So, I recall my hand going back into his; and I sat there with him quietly for a time, spending one of Cap's last hours on earth in some mystical kind of communion with him. I have been forever grateful to Cap for being my teacher that day, showing me so clearly what he wanted and needed from me, a fellow human on this sometimes unpredictable sojourn of life.

Honoring Each Particular Soul, Just Where They Are

Evergreen Hospice in the Puget Sound area has a medical director named Hope Wechkin. What a special name for a doctor/healer to have: As soon as she walks into a room there is Hope! I learned about her through a friend who called me up to let me know about a newspaper article about her that told of the unique work (play) that she does. Besides being a family and palliative care physician, Dr. Hope is a talented musician and actress and performs a one-woman play called "Charisma." This is a play about a seriously ill person in a hospital and the characters she encounters there.

I went to see her show and found it uniquely entertaining. However, what really struck me about Dr. Hope's philosophy is something that was shared in the newspaper article. She commented that when we work with hospice or palliative care, we "jump off the medical train." Then, we evaluate and work "on an individual basis [with] what makes sense for each patient. Instead of telling the body what to do, in terms of routinely ordering tests . . . we let the [particular] body tell us" what is needed. I loved reading these words because I believe this is exactly what spiritual counselors are called to do on hospice as well: We take each person exactly where they are in the moment and help their spirit find what it is they need for their spiritual growth and journey at this time. We must take care not to move into a place of preaching or prescribing what we think the person might need to learn, but rather open-heartedly listen and reflect back what we hear their spirit calling and yearning for. Rather than impose any of our judgments or beliefs on a person as the end of life encroaches, we need to be about helping that individual find what will help him or her "float their spiritual boat." We need to be encouragers of the spiritual life to the highest degree and in a most sensitive and flexible manner.

I recently came across a beautiful poem called "All Souls Day" that speaks about the gentleness with which we need to approach death. Let me allow this magnificent poem to speak for itself:

> Be careful, then, and be gentle about death.
> For it is hard to die, it is difficult to go through
> The door, even when it opens.
> And the poor dead, when they have left the walled
> And silvery city of the now hopeless body
> Where are they to go, Oh where are they to go?
> They linger in the shadow of the earth.
> The earth's long conical shadow is full of souls
> That cannot find the way across the sea of change.
> Be kind, Oh be kind to your dead
> And give them a little encouragement
> And help them to build their little ship of death.
> For the soul has a long, long journey after death
> To the sweet home of pure oblivion.
> Each needs a little ship, a little ship
> And the proper store of meal for the longest journey.
> Oh, from out of your heart
> Provide for your dead once more, equip them
> Like departing mariners, lovingly.
>
> *– D.H. Lawrence* (1885–1930)

Suggested Exercise

Practice: Attentive Listening

Note: This exercise helps to slow down conversations and makes certain that genuine communication is taking place.

Find a partner willing to participate in this exercise with you. Decide on a topic to share with each other. (You could choose to share a meaningful experience you had recently, for example.) Then decide who will speak first. The one who listens first will focus on fully listening to the other. They will simply "receive" whatever the other person is saying as fully as possible, without reacting or responding in any way. If possible, the listener must not even nod their head. Just "be fully present" to the other and simply be a witness with your whole body and being to the other person and to what he or she is saying. Then, after five minutes or so, switch roles. The one who was listening first gets to share, and the one who was speaking first gets to be the listener.

After doing this exercise, reflect on your experience with separating the roles of listening and sharing. You might talk with each other (or write on a sheet of paper) what you learned about yourself as a listener. You might also describe what it was like to receive the gift of attentive listening.

Finding Humor in Death

My Aunt Pat died in January from cancer. She was in her mid 80's. She was a very special person with a deep Christian faith that she applied very practically to life. Near the end of her days in the middle of the night her family – spouse, children, and grandchildren – were gathered around her bed and all prayed for her. She drifted off for a while, and we were all thinking this was the end.

After a while she came to, looked around the room, and said something like, "All that for nothing!" Her grandson, in his 40's, responded to her, "Either you haven't died yet, or you're in a room full of ugly angels." The family all laughed once more together. She died shortly after that.

– Sally Kaiser

I have a story of my own about Aunt Helen's death that reminds me of this one. It's called "Am I Dead Yet?" You'll find it in chapter 6 of *The Last Adventure of Life* (pp. 84-85, 2nd edition).

5

There Is So Much More Than Meets the Eye

"If I had influence with the good fairy who is supposed to preside over the christening of all children, I should ask that her gift to each child in the world be a sense of wonder so indestructible that it would last throughout life."

— *Rachel Carson*

Without a doubt, the biggest lesson I've learned through hospice work is that there is so much more than meets the eye. This is all the more powerful a lesson because of the way our culture emphasizes physical science. We've come to believe, quite erroneously I believe, that unless you can see, touch, hear, or taste something, it's not real. I'd invite you to do hospice work for a year and see if that belief still holds true for you when you've completed the year. I guarantee that after being a hospice volunteer or worker for a year or more, your perspective on life is likely to change significantly. (Thank goodness that the "quantum" perspective is coming into view in science. This is helping us finally link spirituality and science together.)

At its very root, life is a mystery. Therefore, the moments of birth and death are particularly shrouded in mystery. The few days before and after I gave birth to my daughter, Heather, was a time in which I felt I was in some kind of altered space. Everything looked and felt a little different from what it normally felt like – especially the rooms in the hospital in which I gave birth. And I recall the music that we had playing in the room while Heather was being born haunted me for days, even weeks after her birth. At times, I kept hearing the same music that I'd heard on the CD player in the delivery room, even when there was no chance that it could be playing in the area.

Although I've not died yet, nor have I had a near death experience, I would venture to say that the few days before and after a death are particularly shrouded in mystery, especially for the one dying, and sometimes their loved ones, too. I had many mystical things that happened to me or that I heard about on hospice that happened during this numinous time, some of which you can read about in my first book, *The Last Adventure of Life* (see chapter 8 in particular).

One visit with a hospice patient stands out. I had visited with him once or twice already, but this time he was in his bed. He was probably a week or two away from his actual death. After we had been talking for a short while, he asked me, "Who was that woman who came in the room with you?" I wasn't sure how to respond to this because I was not aware of another person having entered his room with me. I asked him questions about the person he had seen, and together we surmised that he had seen an angel or a spirit guide. Perhaps she was getting him prepared for his journey into the next realm; and maybe she had taken the opportunity to materialize in his room with me so as not to frighten him at a different time. I remember being struck by this experience with this man because I had never had anything like that happen before. However, in hospice, I began to realize that anything can happen.

In *The Last Adventure of Life* I share the story of discovering that my late mother and unborn brother were two of my guides in the bereavement work that I did at that time (chapter 8). This information came from a woman who can read spiritual energy and vibration that reside in the aura of a person. Needless to say, my life since that day of learning about this special connection has never been the same. And I find myself looking forward to meeting not only my mother, but also my unborn brother, Stephen, in the spirit world one day.

My Great Aunt Gladys, mentioned earlier, was also a wonderful teacher for me in this regard. Thanks to her, I will always know that there are many mysteries in the world that none of us can fully understand or explain. Unexpected and unexplainable things happen, and these can be celebrated and appreciated just as they are.

> "So we do not lose heart. Even though our outer nature is wasting away, our inner nature is being renewed day by day. For this slight momentary affliction is preparing us for an eternal weght of glory beyond all measure, because we look not at what can be seen but at what cannot be seen; for what can be seen is temporary, but what cannot be seen is eternal."
>
> – II Corinthians 4:16-18

Suggested Exercise

Practice: Write or Journal about Mystical Experiences Related to Your Life

Write down some of the mystical experiences that you have witnessed, or heard about. If you have been close to someone who has died, what were your experiences around that person? What particularly stands out about those experiences? Did they help you unburden your fears around death and the spiritual unknown?

Have you ever witnessed a birth or birthed a child yourself? If so, what mystery do you recall witnessing or experiencing at that time? Write these reflections down and ponder how they could relate to the dying experience – the other end of life's spectrum.

Finding Humor – and Love – in Death

The following story comes from a colleague and fellow author in hospice chaplaincy:

In the Palm of His Hands

It was about one year into my Hospice experience as a Chaplain when I met a man who was an artist and loved to have fun with people around him. I had been visiting this man about two months. We would look at his artistry and reflect on what it had meant to him through the years. As the days grew closer to his death, he became more and more serious with me. He had a deep abiding faith I did not know about until he reached his final days.

We had scheduled visits together each week. On one particular week, Joe asked me to see him which was unusual. I knew something was up. He knew his time was drawing to a close, and he wanted to share something with me. As I was driving over to his home, I remember reviewing some of our visits together. I pondered in my heart just how much of himself he had revealed to me in the last weeks of his life. He moved from a playful artist to a man with a deep reverence for living he finally had words to express.

He had become a part of my life in a heartfelt way. I am not sure he needed to for himself, as much as I believe he was doing this for a young hospice chaplain still growing in his ability to care for a dying person's soul. When I was invited into his home by his wife, she escorted me into the living room where Joe was sitting. She left us there to talk. Joe began to share with me that he knew his time was upon him to die, and he wanted to talk with me. Although this was almost 18 years ago, I still remember Joe looking at me with a serious demeanor. He told me that our relationship meant a great deal to him, and he was very grateful for our time together. At this point, my throat tightened as he brought a tear to my eye. I could tell that Joe wanted to tell me how much he cared for our time together. He said, "Sam, I want you to know that when I die, I am going to put in a good word for you with God." I looked at him in utter shock. Then, I told him in a quiet voice "Thank you Joe." With a slight grin on his face, he told me "Because Sam, you're going to need it." It was then, I knew, I had been had by a great artist.

He got a big laugh out of me on that day, and I knew then that he was on his way to create a masterpiece. Joe knew how to face his own death with the creative imagination he had shared with the world through his ability to bring form to a formless canvass. He painted a memory for me that moved my heart from sorrow to joy. The artistry in this man's soul made me a better man on that day. He created an eternal relationship with me that will never die.

— Sam Oliver, author of *Angel of Promise*

6

Developing Flexibility

Water: The Source of Life
Nothing in the world is as soft and yielding as water,
Yet for dissolving the hard and inflexible,
Nothing can surpass it.
The soft overcomes the hard,
The gentle overcomes the rigid.

— Tao Te Ching

"Blessed are the flexible, for they shall not be bent out of shape."

— author unknown

Working with hospice, I found that I needed to develop a flexible approach, both in the way I physically worked my day, as well as how I approached the variety of people I met. Some days, I would have my day all planned out to visit certain people. But then, when the day came around I would find out that one person had died, another wasn't feeling up to a visit, and so forth. Or sometimes I would need to add a visit with someone who urgently needed a visit that day, so I would have to shift my plans accordingly. In this way, I was constantly prodded to maintain a loose hold on my plans and schedule.

Back in college I'd heard a memorable sermon by the Rev. William Sloan Coffin in which he shared that our lives are made up of the interruptions that occur. We think we have our life or our day all mapped out, and then something can come along and change everything. You've no doubt had days and times in your life like that. Spirit has the room to work with us especially through the changes and interruptions that surface in our lives. So the more we can remain open to Spirit's movement, acknowledging the need to be flexible no matter what's going on in our day or life, the more we leave room to be guided by Spirit.

Here's a true story that happened to me a couple of years ago that illustrates my point: One sunny late summer afternoon I got on my bicycle and rode over to the eleven-circuit beautiful labyrinth at our neighborhood St. Hilda St. Patrick Episcopal church to take a contemplative labyrinth walk. (I've used the labyrinth as a tool for healing and spiritual growth for some time now – see chapter 11 of *The Last Adventure of Life* and my website, www.changewithcourage.com, for much more on a variety of body-mind-spirit healing tools.)

On my way home, I passed a car that had pulled off to the right-hand side of the road. A head popped out of the car and called my name. I could hardly believe who turned out to be in the car: It was the young man Ryan who had been on the Grandmother Drum trip I had taken to Guatemala a few years ago on the Spring Equinox! I knew that Ryan lived with his parents in the south Seattle area, but what were the chances that he and his brother – who had been out on a hike and were on their way home – would find me by synchronistically driving through my north Lynnwood-Mukilteo neighborhood?

Ryan got out of his car and we had a joy-filled reunion. After a lovely chat, I invited the two over for a spaghetti dinner at our place. He and his brother offered to make a trip to the local Safeway to get some food to go with our dinner. My daughter had a few of her friends over for the afternoon, so we ended up sharing a very special, memorable evening altogether. Herein lies the magic of the Universe: We are all interconnected; we are all loved beyond measure and taken care of. Watch, believe in, and intend, expect the miracles to take place in your life (more on this in chapter 10).

In *The Last Adventure of Life*, I shared in the Afterthoughts that water is the symbol for the consciousness we are moving toward in our world right now because it represents flexibility. We are moving from the "two," or dualistic energy to the "three," or all-inclusive goddess energy. This "three energy" is represented by the mystical substance, water. Did you know that water is the only substance in the world that rises to the surface when it freezes? Even our scientists don't completely understand water and how it works. And water is the miraculous substance that allows us to have life on earth in the first place. Its ability to flow with such flexibility is truly remarkable.

Thanks to my many years of learning and growing with my hospice families, I am gradually allowing myself to flow more freely like water in my life, work, and play!

Suggested Exercise

Practice: The Heaven on Earth Meditation

Begin by taking some very deep breaths and getting comfortable in your body. As you take these deep breaths, scan your body and see if there are any places where you have tension or pain. Breathe deeply into any areas of stress or tension and see any stress leaving your body with the out-breath. Imagine bringing light and love to your entire body with your deep, healing breaths.

Now, as you continue taking deep, loving breaths, close your eyes and visualize a tube of light that begins about one hand-length above your head and stretches to about one hand-length below your feet. See the two ends of the tube open. Breathe life through your tube from above and below; and let it meet in your heart area. From there, it will radiate into a sphere around your body. The flow will be continuous on the inhale and the exhale; just allow it to surround you and enlarge you for a minute or two.

Bring your attention to Mother Earth now. You might visualize a favorite place you enjoy in Nature and feel your love for the Mother – for the trees, the birds, the animals, the water, and anything else that comes to mind. Gather these feelings of love into your heart; you might see your love as a colorful sphere of light. After your love for the Mother is gathered into your heart, send it down to the center of the earth, knowing even as you do so that the Mother will be responding by sending her love and energy back to you. Wait until you can feel this energy back from Mother Earth.

Now, place your attention on Father Sky, on all life in the cosmos, where inspiration comes from. Feel your love for all the stars and galaxies, and all life in the heavens. Sense the love you have for the Father; you might imagine looking into a night sky. Then take all of your love for the Father and gather it into your heart area. See that love as a sphere of light and send it up to Father Sky. As you send your love to the Father know that Father Sky will be sending his love back to you as well. Then wait until you actually feel the love of the Father returning to bless you. It could be helpful to visualize a column of golden light coming down over your torso as a way to help organize the energy coming up from Mother Earth.

Now, visualize the love of Mother Earth and the blessings of Father Sky mixing and blessing you and the aura around your body. You could see the different colors of energy blending around your body. And know that now the holy trinity is mystically present in you – the Mother, the Father, and the Holy Child. This means that something very special can take place.

Visualize the tube that stretches through your body again. Now, place your attention on the opposite ends. Open up the ends even further, and allow all life everywhere to enter from both ends, to enter into your heart, and to radiate as light all around you. Open up the ends, and allow God/Goddess/All That Is to come in and to form a sphere of love and light around your body.

Now, as you experience your whole being being blessed, and as you slowly allow the sphere around you to expand, gradually visualize the energy moving out toward your neighbors and local community. You might think of someone to whom you'd like to send this loving, joy-filled energy. Visualize sending it to that person, or family, or community of people who could particularly benefit from it. Keep letting the energy expand, allowing it to get bigger and bigger, moving out into the world faster and faster. If you can, in the end, let it expand uncontrollably throughout all dimensions and in all directions. Allow it to return back to all life, everywhere, blessing and bringing peace and delight wherever it goes.

May peace prevail on earth. May peace prevail among all religions, too.

Finding Joy and Freedom in the Moment of Death

"At the moment of utter solitude, when the body breaks down on the edge of infinity, a separate time begins to run that cannot be measured in any normal way. In the course of several days sometimes, with the help of another presence that allows despair and pain to declare themselves, the dying seize hold of their lives, take possession of them, unlock their truth. They discover the freedom of being true to themselves. It is as if, at the very culmination, everything managed to come free of the jumble of inner pains and illusions that prevent us from belonging to ourselves…

"… Death can cause a human being to become what he or she was called to become. It can be, in the fullest sense of the word, an accomplishment."

– Francois Mitterrand, in *Intimate Death – How the dying teach us how to live*, by Marie de Hennezel

7

Growing Our Intuition

"Be still. Breathe. Know — you are fine."
                                        — *Jodie Preston, M.D.*

We are living in tumultuous times. It seems that just about everything and everyone on the planet is experiencing some kind of transition these days. As a human species we are moving through a shift in consciousness. This is not always easy, and the more we resist the process, the more difficult it becomes. It is as if we are all "on hospice," learning to let go of and die to an old model of living that in many ways is no longer serving us. If we can acknowledge this and begin to let go, the way will open for us. But if we resist and fight the letting go process, we will make it doubly hard for ourselves.

In my own life during the last few years I have been challenged to reexamine my diet, especially my sugar and caffeine intake. If I can keep a primarily good and healthy diet for myself, I do well. However, whenever I start to go back to my old, not so healthy habits, I seem to have to pay a price. The old habits take a toll on my body.

There's a kind of parallel going on in my mental and

emotional life as well: My old habit of judging myself and other people no longer works very well. This only brings on more fear and judgment. Rather, my heart wants to be open and accepting of who we are as people in this moment. Instead of judging myself and others, my heart wants to love and acknowledge what a wonderful, miraculous soul each one of us is. We are blessed to be here on earth, each making our way, at our own speed, toward the greatness of who we really are.

Our higher selves (souls) create all kinds of scenarios that we are called to move through to grow and learn and hopefully transform. I heard a meaningful definition of a successful life recently through Eva Ravenwood who's written the book *The Next God*. The definition is "to be able to make progress on our spiritual path."

What I'm noticing is that whatever direction our intuition is moving us toward is the direction we need to be moving in. Our own personal and unique intuition – connected to our "Beloved I Am" selves – is our best guide, perfect for each one of us. And the best way we connect with our intuition is to create spaces in our lives when we can actually "tune in" to that still small voice of God/dess calling out to us and instilling us with inspiration and information.

I have heard it said that all of us on the planet today are growing in our intuition and psychic abilities. This is related to the fact that the frequency on the planet is rising and we are moving to a higher octave spiritually and vibrationally speaking. Even as I write this, it is snowing outside and there's been snow on the ground in the Puget Sound for over ten days. This is unheard of, and our whole nation is experiencing a kind of deep freeze right over the winter solstice and holy-day season (and all the holy days seemed to have converged this year). Some of my friends have been commenting about what a perfect opportunity we are all being shown at this time – to move away from the materialistic frenzy that tends to take over at this time of year. Instead, we are being called to tune into the beauty and love of life itself, the magic of the earth, snow, and of our soul's yearning to honor the life within.

Here is a story from my hospice work that shares how I was shown the grace of flexibility and intuition in the dying process: Douglas, my hospice patient, had been struggling to breathe all night long. In fact, breathing had become the major issue in his life during the last week. He was now wearing an oxygen mask. His daughter, Marcia, was on one side of his hospital bed; his granddaughter, Jessica, on the other. They had just tucked him back into bed after a sleepless night on the Hospice Unit. Later, I found out they'd both been giving him permission to let go all night long, for he was suffering too much.

It was a Monday morning, and I had just listened to my voice mails. One of our palliative care specialist nurses had left me a message saying that Douglas wanted me to come and anoint him with the essential oils as I had done for him the previous week. Driving toward the hospice house on the Eastside of Puget Sound, I had no idea that I was about to witness one of the most profound experiences I've ever had as a spiritual counselor with the essential oils.

Having revamped my schedule for the day, I entered Douglas's room with my essential oils and a favorite CD of East/West chants called *Dream Chants east & west* (Cynthia Snodgrass) in hand. I felt some power beyond my own guiding me. Upon entering Douglas's room, I knew what needed to be done: First, I anointed him with some oils. Marcia and Jessica, who had been expecting me, made room for me to bless their father and grandfather with the oils. I got out myrtle, the Believe blend, and frankincense. I lifted the oxygen mask and let Douglas smell the Believe blend. After anointing the area

around his nose and lungs with the Believe oil, I rubbed some
myrtle on his right ribcage and some on his feet. Then, I went
up to his forehead and anointed his head with frankincense,
my favorite oil. I've discovered that frankincense, meaning
"real incense," is also the favorite incense of the spirit realm.

The oils almost immediately had an effect. Douglas's
breathing slowed down and his whole body began to relax.
Next, I went over to the CD player and got the beautiful chants
by Cynthia Snodgrass filling the room with their special
harmony (*Ubi karitas et amour* … "Where God is, there love
is …"). Douglas's oxygen mask had been removed, and it was
Marcia who noticed that Douglas had opened his eyes to look
straight up, above his bed.

"He's going, he's going!" she exclaimed.

"Well, maybe," I thought to myself, as one never really
knows when and how the dying process will happen. Hospice
staff learn to respect that final transitions have a mind of their
own.

I also found myself actively praying at this point. I recall
offering a prayer out loud, too, around Douglas's bed with his
two beloved ones. Before long, Douglas's breathing had slowed
down even more, and it became clear that he was in the final
stages of letting go. The three of us witnessing this turn of
events were so amazed, it did not even occur to us to leave the
room. Within twenty minutes of my entering his room and
administering the oils, Douglas had taken his last breath.

After a few minutes of experiencing this sacred time
together, one of us left the room to go find a nurse. Two hospice
staff came into Douglas's room to help us begin to digest what
had just happened. After confirming that Douglas had died,
they checked his limbs, noting that there had been none of
the mottling that usually happens before a person dies. In
hindsight, I believe Douglas realized that the relaxation offered

him by the essential oils gave him an opportunity to let go and make his way to the next realm. This meant that he could forgo the usual process of the body slowing down gradually. Perhaps when he'd gazed up above his bed he had seen his recently deceased daughter as Marcia had surmised, and this gave him further impetus to join her, merging with Spirit as swiftly as possible.

Needless to say, this experience opened me up to the subtle yet tremendous power that essential oils can have in the end-of-life and dying process. On some level I have known that the oils possess this kind of power, since I've heard about how they were used in ancient times around death and burial. After all, it was the three wise men who brought Jesus frankincense and myrrh. The Egyptians were known for their use of these oils in their tombs and pyramids as well.

Incidentally, one doesn't have to be dying or experiencing a transition to enjoy the benefits of these oils. I use them on a regular basis, to lift my mood and raise my vibration: Frankincense is known for its anti-depressant quality as it has the ability to connect a person with the spiritual realm; it is also a wonderful tonic for the skin and anti-tumoral as well. I heard about a mother who had a son with a brain tumor. She kept her son's head wet with frankincense. Over time the son was healed by the power of this oil that was once considered more valuable than gold. Frankincense has also been known to work its magic with people suffering from Alzheimer's disease. If ever you happen to be with an obstinate person who suffers from Alzheimer's, all you need do is apply some of this wonderful oil to your own hands. Then, spend at least a few minutes in close proximity to the person. This will soon have a calming effect on the headstrong individual.

Suggested Exercise
*Practice: Meditation – Begin to Develop a Regular
Practice in Your Life*

Take a few minutes each day to just sit quietly and listen.
If you cannot do this every day, then start by taking five to
twenty minutes two or three times a week. If you cannot sit
and listen, then walk or run outside and listen, or use the
treadmill and listen, or simply give yourself time and space
to gaze out the window. The point is to take the time to
simple be, and put aside your busy life. Our busyness and
achievement-oriented way of life has gotten the better of us,
and we have lost the art of gently being with ourselves and
one another.

Give yourself this gift of paying attention inwardly and you
will likely be surprised; you will very possibly begin to notice
things you never noticed before – like which way the wind
is blowing, or where and when the animals and birds come
around you. As you tune in to another level of being, you will
find nature and other aspects of life speaking to you. You will
begin to notice the "signs" that show up for you. Life comes to
have a special, rather magical quality about it!

Finding the Humor in Death

Death Humor Scottish Style

It is a fact of life that the Grim Reaper will call on every one of us one day, and when that day comes it is time to say bye-bye cruel world.

Grief is a strange thing that affects different people in different ways: some people curl up into a corner and wish the world away, some people hide how they are feeling and explode a long time later down the line, others use humor to help get them through the death of a loved one.

The following is dedicated to the people who use humor to help get them through.

Top 10 Sayings to Death

In Scotland there are many old sayings that are related to death which are humorous and guaranteed to liven up the most boring wakes.

10) Death – the last sleep? No, it is the final awakening.

9) Be happy while you're living, for you're a long time dead.

8) Dead men are free men.

7) There isn't a cure for death.

6) Death pays off all debts.

5) Better wade back mid water than go forward and drown.

4) Better live in hope than die in despair.

3) Better be a coward than a corpse.

2) A thread will tie an honest man better than a rope will do a rogue.

1) I DO HOPE HE IS DEAD, THEY BURIED HIM THIS MORNING!

There is a little rhyme that is common in Scotland that is often said if someone takes a coughing fit:

"It's not the cough that carries you off: it's the coffin they carry you off in!"

– *Found on the Internet, at* www.hubpages.com

8

Holding a Grateful Heart and a Nonjudgmental Attitude

"The long era of judgment has been man's darkest night, but that will end soon when the last judgment has been made. The last judgment will be the judgment against judgment itself. At that time, human consciousness at last will rise in splendor like a valiant bridegroom to join his bride, the Sacred Heart. This is the Holy Wedding which has been the dream of prophets. After this marriage occurs, there will be peace on Earth. In the meantime, it is your right to seek a betterment of life in all the ways that are available to you. Enjoy every opportunity for positive change. Make the most of every day."

— Jesus, through Glenda Green

I have learned that the power of unconditional love speaks volumes at the time that death draws near. Rather than expressing judgment and critical thinking as our culture tends to do, I have found that the end of life is a time to release judgment and share pure, unadulterated love with the one who is reviewing his or her life one last time. There is a beautiful poem by Doug Smith called "Do Not Judge Death" that speaks volumes in this regard:

Do Not Judge Death
Death can be very painful.
Do not waver in your attitude of allowing.
Death can be very exhausting.
Do not waver in your attitude of allowing.

Death can be very ugly.
Do not waver in your attitude of allowing.

Childbirth can be very painful, exhausting, and ugly.
Yet a beautiful child can still be born.
So it is with dying.

Do not judge the death by the dying!
Do not judge the dying!
Do not judge death!
Do not judge!

Be prepared for anything.
Allow for anything.
Accept anything.
There is no other way.
 — *The Tao of Dying: A Guide to Caring,*
 by Doug Smith (1994)

As I faced another's mortality and therefore my own as well through doing hospice work, I found myself reflecting: How can I help myself and the one I sit with out of the fear, fear of the unknown, or fear of fear itself? I have heard it said and then confirmed through personal experience that two of the fastest ways out of fear are to be in thanksgiving and to create. When we develop a grateful heart by focusing on the things we are grateful for in our lives, fear dissipates. Also, when we can make the space to create what we love and what we are good at, fear tends to move out. When I find myself in fear, I do my best to write in my gratitude journal or nudge myself to get back into playing an instrument I love. The main thing is to do something that I love to do, and create while I'm at it.

Another way to leave fear behind is to cultivate love. As a caregiver, I've learned that it's especially important to give myself the gift of love. Here are some ideas that have helped me: First, make space for deep grieving in my own life, in a creative and self-nurturing way. For example, I can just take a day to "be" and allow myself to feel my feelings for a while. Combining this with walking, yoga, or an exercise of some kind can be helpful, too. Or I might take the time and space to honor the memory of someone I love and miss in my life.

Second, as much as possible, I need to forgive myself for all the mistakes, heartaches, and resentments I haven't let go of yet. As a caregiver and oldest daughter, I've discovered how sometimes very hard I am on myself; and it's so important to have compassion toward me. (See chapter 6 of *The Last Adventure of Life* and the links on my website for tools for forgiveness and letting go.)

Third, I have found deep nourishment from developing a spiritual practice that includes tools such as meditation, music, and a deep breathing exercise. This works best when I practice it as often as I can, daily for a short time, if possible.

Finally, it's so important to let myself know how much I love myself. I've learned a practice in which I face my bathroom mirror every morning and evening and say the words "I love you, Dancing Heart!" to myself over and over again. I've been learning that, in actuality, I cannot love myself too much.

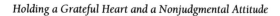

"As we count our blessings, we literally bathe ourselves inwardly in good hormones. And ... a sense of appreciation ... will make us feel better!"

— M.J. Ryan

Suggested Exercise

Practice: The Gratitude Journal

Get out a pen or pencil and a notepad, and begin making a list of the things that you are grateful for in your life. Write down anything that comes to mind. After you've exhausted your list, let it go and give thanks for this day – another gift of life. You might want to make this a habit from day to day, or week to week. Gratitude is a wonderful way out of fear.

Finding Humor in Death

Perhaps you've heard the old story that goes like this. It may be a little sacrilegious for some, but fun: In life there are really only two things to worry about – whether you are healthy or whether you are sick. If you are healthy then there is nothing to worry about, but if you are sick there are only two things to worry about – whether you will get better or die. If you get better, well there is nothing to worry about, but if you die you only have two things to worry about – whether you will go to heaven or hell. If you go to heaven, well, there is nothing to worry about; but if you go to hell – well, you will be so busy shaking hands with old friends that you won't have time to worry!

– Author unknown, found on the Internet

9

Being Open to the Mystery and Unpredictability of Life

"I would love to live
Like a river flows,
Carried by the surprise
Of its own unfolding."
— John O'Donohue

A lovely synchronistic reconnection happened to me recently. My daughter and I were on a long anticipated trip to the Big Island of Hawaii. Glancing up to look at the departure time for our flight to the Big Island on the electronic screen, I literally "ran into" a friend from Seattle who I hadn't seen in months at the San Francisco airport. He was heading to the Big Island, too, in the midst of caring for his 94-year-old mother who was receiving hospice care. As we talked further about his situation a few days later over some lunch, my friend shared with me that he had made a rather magical connection with a well respected emergency care doctor in a coffee shop earlier last year. As soon as this doctor – first name, Shay – heard that my friend was caring for his dying mother, she shared with him the following four things:

1) You are on a severe learning curve;

2) No one can predict what will happen (despite many who think they can!);

3) You are under more stress than you think you are; and

4) You must do things to take care of your stress, both for you and for the sake of your mother whom you are caring for.

My friend acknowledged that he has used this doctor's wise words as his mantra as he's been caring for his mother over the course of the year. His mother is very close to death now, and the words still ring true for him. They ring true for me as well. And they move me toward reflecting on the last days of my own mother's life.

I have been enjoying watching the turning of the seasons in beautiful color these autumn days. Some of the trees have amazingly brilliant, gorgeous colors; they're captivating! These autumn leaves remind me of how often, in people's lives, too, there's that last hurrah, a final burst of energy expressed just before a person lets go and transitions into the next world.

I think back to almost twenty years ago now, when my own mother was dying. She was being cared for at home, by my sister Linda and some very generous women from her Lutheran church in Camp Hill, PA. Essentially, she had been lying in bed and not doing much for two weeks. Linda, who'd been with her for the duration thanks to an understanding supervisor, called up my other sister and me on a Friday to let us know that she felt the time was close for Mom's death. She suggested that we both make the trip out to see her if we wanted to say our final goodbyes.

My sister and I both made it "home" the next day, on Saturday before Father's Day, to be with our mother. She was still alert enough to greet us and spend some time honoring us with her energy and love, even though there were very few words shared at that point. Although Mom was not eating much, she shared a bite of *zaru soba* – Japanese buckwheat noodles with a dipping sauce, often served cold in the summer time – one of her favorite Japanese dishes that had been prepared for the gathered family. Dad made the comment "Something's keeping you going, Betty," and my mom opened her eyes wide and spoke one word, "LOVE!" I remember having a strong feeling of her essence that day, something like having the layers of an onion skin peeled away and the core essence of who she really was remaining at the center. I was privy to experiencing that essence of who my mother truly was and still treasure it.

The next morning, on Father's Day, which also happened to be my father's fortieth ordination anniversary day, my mother awoke saying that she wanted to attend church with us. Unfortunately, in her physical condition there was no way to get mom to church that morning, even though she and Dad were living next to the church in the parsonage. As soon as we all got back from church, however, we were able to get Mom out of bed and into the living room for an informal indoor picnic. Then, right on cue, a couple that my parents had known and loved for many years showed up at their doorstep to say hello. They joined our "picnic" and there was more laughter and joyful energy shared. That evening I recall thinking: Wow, Mom seems to be getting her energy back. Maybe she'll be able to live another week?

On the following Monday morning my mother took her last breath around eight-thirty. Clearly, she had rallied the last remaining energy she had for all of us, and on our father's special day. What a gift! And what profound beauty we can share with one another, right up until the very last breath of this earthly life.

I honor the beauty of the leaves as I honor the beauty of my mother's soul.

Suggested Exercise

Practice: Change Your Subconscious (in four minutes) Exercise

Cross one of your ankles over the other one. Now stretch out your arms and cross the opposite arm over the other arm, bringing your hands together, folding them in prayer position with your arms twisted. Then bend your elbows and moving your hands beneath your elbows, tucking them inside your chest.

Now notice your tongue: Make sure that it is touching the roof of your mouth as you take some deep breaths. As you exhale, whisper to yourself what you would like to have in your life in the day/time ahead. You might whisper "I am joy"; "I am grateful"; or "I am at peace." You are training your subconscious with these words.

Keep repeating the breathing pattern with the whispering of your phrase for two minutes.

Then, switch everything out. Cross the opposite ankle over your other ankle; and do the same thing with your arms after reversing them. Then continue to whisper the same phrase to yourself as you take deep breaths for two minutes.

Now you have retrained your subconscious mind to be how you would like to be in the next day or period of time. Enjoy the results.

Finding Humor in Death

The doctors are in the room with a sleeping patient who everyone believes is sleeping, and a fly is buzzing around the room. They get tired of it, grab the defib paddles and shock the fly... dead fly. Holding the paddles over the (now) dead man, the doc says "well that killed him" just as the family walks in the room.

They played this video as an introduction to a lecture in (nursing) school a couple of weeks ago. It was a good attention grabber.

— Author unknown, found on the Internet

10

We Are All Profoundly Interconnected: Tuning in to the Synchronicity and Magic of Life

"There are two ways to live your life. One is as though nothing is a miracle. The other is as though everything is a miracle."

– Albert Einstein

During the early years of my work with hospice, my marriage was going through hard times. Eventually Peter and I divorced and my eight-year-old daughter and I were able to move into a brand-new condominium. I will never forget something that happened one day soon after moving into the condo with Heather.

Heather and I had been to the mall to purchase some seed beads for the first time. We had some beautiful Celtic music on in the car and were driving into the driveway of our new home. Heather was holding the bag with the newly purchased beads, enjoying running the string of beads over her hands. Suddenly, she piped up, "Listening to this music and feeling these beads, I'm remembering the time I was on earth when there were no tall buildings." She proceeded to say that she recalled women like Starfeather and other healer and ceremonialist women we knew. She reported they were with her in that lifetime. Then, her heart opened and she wept, saying how much she missed that time on earth. She became so emotional that I began to tear up with her, sensing somehow that I might well have been with her then.

Even before this deeply emotional experience with Heather, I was developing a sense that despite my Christian belief system, reincarnation made sense to me. I'd been waking up to the fact that there was probably a good reason I felt deep connections with certain people and places, even after only one or two encounters. Hearing this unsolicited statement out of the blue from little Heather made it crystal clear to me that we have been here on earth before, and chances are pretty good that we will be back again someday in the future.

The beautiful thing about my experience of spending time with the dying has been that I have grown and been deeply transformed by it. First of all, I have become more comfortable with the act of *being* in a culture of dying people. This has been such a gift in our busy culture. I have also found that I've lessened the load of fear for myself around death and grief. I believe that I have also strengthened my intuition while spending time with dying people and their families. I seem to pay more attention to my inner life because the emphasis is more on being rather than doing; at times I have found myself more comfortable being quiet with the person who is dying – rather like being in deep meditation with them.

By spending time with one who is gravely ill, I have also been taught the gift of living more fully in the present moment. Because I was allowed to become more aware of the gift of each moment, I have become more aware of the present, with all its joy, peace, and potential for humility, gratitude, and curiosity. While spending time with one whose time is short, I have become more aware of the gift of time that I have. I no longer take time for granted as much and have begun to naturally open up to less judgment and more love in my life. You could say that my heart is more open since working with the dying.

Sometimes the dying can bless you with the most surprising wisdom. One day, I was visiting a gracious woman who was suffering from cancer and dementia. She had been a beautician most of her long life. It was difficult for me to believe that this lovely woman had dementia because she could keep up with our conversations so easily. I brought up the topic of death with her as a way to open the conversation one day. On our next visit, she let me know indirectly through her loving family that she did not want our conversations to be about death. However, on this day that we were visiting, she just popped out with the words: **"It's a great life if you don't weaken; it's a great death if you don't stiffen."**

Curiously, neither her family nor I could come up with a clue of how or where she'd come up with this wisdom. Yet to this day I find her words deeply echoing in my soul.

On another occasion, I learned that one of my hospice folk happened to be a poet and a mystic – on her deathbed. I had been visiting her for months, but it was only when she could no longer speak and I was conversing with her family that I learned that she had written poetry during her life. Her family shared a poem that she had written about her destination at the time of death. Ironically, she wrote this poem a few years before she died, though she struggled until close to the end to make peace with that destination:

"Resting"

Peace is upon me,
a soft blanket
of loving and caring,
placed there
by the Lord
there is a prayer within me
and music
enfolding me
a vision of Heaven to come
is faint and barely seen
through eyes that
are dimming
but the vision
that is my soul
sees you,
feels you,
hears you, Lord
that you, Jesus,
for these quiet moments
within the grief and sorrow
that is the shattered world
that surrounds me
peace is upon me,
the silence of an ending life
thank you, Lord,
for Heaven,
my destination.

— Muriel G., May 6, 2006

Suggested Exercise

Practice: Circle of Love Meditation

This is a guided meditation I learned through Jamal Rahman, a Muslim, Sufi, interfaith minister, and my hypnotherapy teacher in Seattle.

Take some deep breaths, close your eyes, and relax. When you have reached a state of deep relaxation, see yourself in your mind's eye walking on a path. The soul loves beauty, so see yourself on a beautiful path in Mother Earth. This could be a path you've walked before, or it could be a brand new path you create through your imagination. As you walk this path of beauty, be aware of your senses: Notice the color, the sounds. . . birds chirping in the air, bees and insects humming, or tree leaves rustling in the wind. Notice the smells and the touch of the earth under your feet.

In time, you will come to a clearing – your special place of beauty. Again, this may be a place you've been before, or it may be a new place, one you create with the parts of nature that you particularly enjoy. If you love water, you might see a body of water there, or a waterfall or creek. If you love trees, you might find a circle of trees there. Perhaps there's a meadow full of your favorite wildflowers with the colors that make your heart sing.

Once you are in your specific spot, sit down in the beauty and simply enjoy it. Again, notice your senses and feel the beauty in your bones. (pause)

After you have become comfortable and oriented here, you can start to see a Circle of Love coming to bless you in this specific place. Use your imagination to see who comes in to

61

bless and support you at this time. There might be family members and friends from this earth plane. There may be loved ones from the Other Side. There may be spiritual guides or angels, or your favorite figures from fairy tales. There could be pets or your beloved animal friends, sometimes known as your "power animals."

Acknowledge each one who comes into your Circle of Love. Everyone is here to support and nourish you. Look them in the eyes and thank them for coming. One or more of them may have a message for you. Receive the message with deep gratitude. Keep going around the circle, noticing who shows up. You are so blessed and loved. Feel the love and support here. You are cherished beyond your knowing. (pause for one to five minutes)

Gradually now, when you are ready, it is time to say goodbye to your Circle of Love. Knowing that you can come here again and bask in your Circle of Love any time you'd like, go around the circle and thank each one who came to support you. If you wish, give them a hug or a kiss as a farewell greeting. Feel your deep and abiding connection with each one.

When you are finished saying your goodbyes to everyone, it's time to return. When you are ready, see yourself back on the path of beauty by which you came here. Enjoy the return walk, noticing the sights and sounds along the way. Mother Earth is nourishing and blessing you with her love, too. (pause)

When you are ready, gradually prepare to come back to this room and reality: You might wiggle your toes or stretch your arms. Eventually you may open your eyes and return to this current reality, with gratitude and love in your heart.

Finding Humor in Death

When I was taking care of a dying woman the family brought in a photo of the patient in her earlier years. Out comes: "She's drop dead gorgeous"! Lucky the family had a sense of humor.

Another patient of mine had an unresolvable bowel obstruction. When her doctor told her there was nothing else he could do for her, she just said to let her die – immediately. It amazes me when people get this news and they are just ready to die right away. They were Italian; and they decided that they would bring in a bottle of wine that evening and have a drink together since she wasn't going home and the doctor okayed it. The wine went in and came out her NG tube! The nursing supervisor was horrified when she found out about it.

– Author unknown, found on the Internet

"What we have once enjoyed and deeply loved we can never lose, for all that we love deeply becomes a part of us."
— *Helen Keller*

11

Healing Tools for Self-care and Relaxation

"Do I remember at every moment that I am dying, and everyone and everything else is, and so treat all beings at all times with compassion [beginning with myself]?"
— *Sogyal Rinpoche*

One of the most important things we can do, especially as caregivers and healers in the area of end-of-life and grief care is to take very good care of ourselves. Too often, caregivers and people who are grieving get so caught up in caring for others and taking care of the day-to-day business of life that they forget to properly care for themselves. Hence, there is a very high burn-out rate for caregivers. I even heard recently at a hospice event that according to one study, the quality of life of caregivers tends to be lower than the quality of life of the patients they care for!

As difficult as it may be, caregivers must learn to love and give to themselves first. Unless they take very good care of themselves first, they will not be able to care well over the long haul for the ones they serve. (*Grace and Grit,* by Ken and Treya Wilber, is a powerful story about a caregiver and his soulmate. Ken cared for Treya diligently and tenaciously, despite many challenges, over the course of their five-year marriage.)

Here are some very simple suggestions of ways to relax and take good care of yourself in the midst of the changes and the care giving that you may be doing for others:

1. Sit or lie down and take some very deep breaths. (If it helps for you to count, count to 4, or 6, or even 8 for the in-breath – then repeat for the out-breath.)

2. Turn on some of your favorite music – harp music, or most instrumental music is wonderful for relaxing – and really listen to it. My daughter made me a CD with some of my favorite pieces on it; it lifts my mood every time I listen to any part of it.

3. Hold each of your fingers for three to five minutes each, preferably in combination with the exercises above.
   > Thumb: To feel secure
   > Index: To release fear
   > Middle: To release anger
   > Ring: To release grief and draw in comfort
   > Pinkie: To release denial and confusion

   (There is a youtube about this is on the home page of Maria's website: **www.changewithcourage.com**.)

4. Go for a walk – or just get outside – in one of your favorite places in nature. If you can find a labyrinth* in your neighborhood, even better; walk it. It is sure to nourish you!

---

* For more about the labyrinth, see pp. 202-203 of *The Last Adventure of Life*. It is an ancient tool for healing that is being resurrected around the world.

5. Get out the lavender oil, or any favorite essential oil that you enjoy, and have fun massaging it onto your fingers, your face, your forehead, and main energy/meridian points. (Maria has a collection of Young Living Essential Oils that she sells, which you can learn more about on her website – the "Essential (YL) Oils" link.

   The 5ml bottles Maria offers are Healing (her special blend of lavender, frankincense, and jojoba), Valor, Believe, PanAway, Joy, and Thieves blends. These are all $10 a bottle. The other two, Harmony and White Angelica blends are $13 a bottle. To order, call: (888) 409-1678, or contact Maria through her website.

6. Cuddle up next to your favorite person, pet, or stuffed animal and take some deep breaths. Hugs of all kinds are always good for relaxation.

7. Practice yoga, tai chi, or Qigong, or find some dance or exercise with slow and easy movements and stretches that work for you. You might consider taking a class in something new and different. Create a fun and healthy "adventure" for yourself!

8. Make your favorite cup of tea and savor the experience of drinking every drop of it.

9. Alkalize your body by eating healthy foods (Call or e-mail Maria for a brochure on this.)

10. Lie down, close your eyes, and picture yourself in a beautiful setting. As you take some deep breaths, see yourself becoming rejuvenated and healed. (Add some of the above ideas to this process, like deep breathing, or putting on some essential oils beforehand.)

11. Rub your hands together and feel the energy between your hands. As you leave your left hand open to receiving the healing/spiritual energy, place your right hand on an

area of your body that needs healing. You might add color to the experience: See the energy moving through your hands as gold, white, pink, or blue/purple. Or, choose your own favorite color that you know will bring you the healing energy you desire.

12. Bind it all together, expressing and feeling deep emotions of gratitude and love, perhaps while you soak in a nice warm bath! Ponder and then write a list of all the things in your life that you appreciate right now. Also, picture all the people, animals, and spiritual helpers who have come into your life. All have come for a reason. And most of them you can appreciate, for one reason or another. Stretch your imagination, and bless every one of them. You could add to this exercise writing about what you would like to have come to you. You might start your sentences with "Wouldn't it be lovely if . . ."

Here are a few more suggestions:

Maria recommends that you have a **Heart Wall Healing**. This is "more than a massage" where you get to release old, negative emotions that are stuck in your 'heart wall' and/or auric field. It can be done in person or long distance. See "Heart Wall Healing" page on Maria's website, or e-mail/call Maria to request a brochure.

See Maria's articles at **Examiner.com (http://tinyurl.com/msv6aw)**. You will find many body-mind-spirit related ideas to help you relax and other articles on grief and healing.

For more information on relaxation and healing techniques see my websites, **www.changewithcourage.com**, **www.soulbaskets.com**, and links at **www.changewithcourage.com/links.htm**.

Suggested Exercise

Practice one of the twelve suggested exercises listed in this chapter – or a combination of them – as often as possible. Keep an open mind and heart, and know that you are so precious and loved beyond measure! May you know each and every day, more and more, how very special you are. And may you remember to take very good care of yourself, always.

Finding Peace and Hope in a Quiet Place

The Cable TV Guy: An Extraordinary Young Man

My Story:

It was just an ordinary morning as I set out on my usual ordinary walk down the ordinarily quiet rainforest road. Lost in my own thoughts, my reverie was broken when a saw a Cable TV truck lumbering up the hill. I wondered about its unordinary presence. Soon enough the same truck – mission apparently accomplished – departed. Curious, I decided to stop the driver. What was the trouble? Why did he stop on my property? He became defensive (in a West Indian sort of way) when I questioned him; until he realized I was merely wondering if we were having some line troubles I wasn't aware of. And then in some mysterious unordinary way – known only to spirit – the following story emerged.

His story:

"I was sent to install a Cable TV and telephone at a number 4 Mt. Washington. I was lost and could not find which house to go to. I drove up the hill next to yours looking for the correct house. What I found instead was this incredible view of the most beautiful property from across the way. Driving back down the hill and still searching, I went up the driveway next to this lovely property and was redirected by an unseen voice to the house below.

My work did not take long this morning so I had some time on my hands. And then you stopped me and then you offered to show me the entrance gate to the labyrinth and the Mt. Washington gardens. And then I discovered a peace I had never known."

"How much does it cost to visit here?" he asked.

He was told, "Nothing." (Although I secretly wanted to say, "It might cost you everything.")

Together we walked up and looked down upon the labyrinth. "Your property is a place for me to feel," he said. "It could be a place for me to write poetry. It is a place I want to bring some special people in my life. This place would not be for most of my friends who live next to me in the housing project. One of my friends, though, is a musician and I know he would love this place. I could not bring a girl right now; any girls I know would not understand.

I have a lot going on in my life; but when I was at your residence I felt trouble free. In 20 minutes I feel my life has changed. I want to talk to my mother and see if she will come out with me to walk the labyrinth. She and I argue a lot and I know something deep down is bothering her. Thank you for stopping me; you made my day. I will return."

– *Nancy Ayer, Veriditas Certified Labyrinth Facilitator*

> *"More than ever it is time for each of us on the planet to awaken to our mortality and our spiritual nature. We need to live with more awareness of how we affect others and the interconnectedness of all. As we each begin to heal ourselves from the inside out, we become a part of healing the Earth and all others on the planet."*
>
> – Maria Dancing Heart

Conclusion: A Vision of Peace

Having been born and raised in Japan and finding myself a kind of bridge between the East and the West, and having been involved in spiritual work for most of my life, I have always had a yearning for peace among the nations and people of world. The vision that I am developing is three-fold:

1) A world in which humanity shares and holds the vibration of peace;

2) A world in which humans no longer fear death.

3) A world in which different cultures and peoples respect and learn from one another's religions and cultures.

One of the main reasons we have conflicts and wars in the world is because we are not doing our grief work in a good way. Often, people are not even aware of the grief that we carry around with us. As humans come to understand, face, and deal with our grief in a meaningful way, we can come to be more peaceful, mature human beings. And working through our issues around death and grief – two sides of the same coin – is paramount.

My vision for the world encompasses a perspective in which when death draws near, we can come to recognize that the dying person has accomplished what he or she has come to do and is now getting ready to graduate from his or her experience on earth. We might even substitute the word "graduation" for "death." The end of life is a time for us to help the dying person celebrate what they have accomplished and learned in the course of their life.

My vision for the world also embraces a time when the different and varied religions of the world will be appreciated and respected for what they are: part of the beautiful tapestry of the rich spirituality encompassing the world.

I would like to close with a vision that I found in Elizabeth Gilbert's book *Eat, Pray, Love*. It is a vision that comes through the Hopi people; and it has stayed with me ever since I read about it. I believe the time for its manifestation is now: The world's religions each contain a spiritual thread. These threads are constantly seeking each other, like long lost lovers, desiring to join and merge as One. When all these threads are finally woven together, they will create a sturdy rope that will pull humanity out of the dark cycle of history that we have been stuck in. In this way, we will create peace on earth.

This reminds me of the echo of voices prophesying the peace that is coming in our time. I've been hearing from around the world that peace is on its way. For instance, James Twyman speaks about a very young, differently-abled Japanese boy who said a few years ago that "Peace is coming soon!" It is said that the Mayan calendar "ends" in 2012, so some are predicting that the world is likely to be different in some major ways sometime around the end of 2012 and the beginning of 2013. Many religions, including the Mormons, have prophesies that peace will return to the earth about this time.

When we look at the world today, it's possible to interpret the future in a variety of ways. Some may think that things are "going down the tubes" in a negative way. However, if we can see this time of chaos and breakdown as a birthing time, we can hold a bigger and wider vision that life is gradually growing and improving on the planet. Sometimes, things can look much worse than they actually are – just before the dawning of a transformative time of rebirth. I choose to believe that human consciousness is steadily rising, and out of the ashes – the death of the old – the phoenix shall rise again.

Suggestions for Death Care Reform in America

1. Face our fears about death – go deeper into our spiritual practice – and find ways to overcome them.

2. Give ourselves and others as much permission to grieve as possible. It is healing to cry, express frustration, shock, sorrow, and all kinds of emotions when we grieve. It's best not to put a time limit on grieving, either. Everyone's different in how we grieve; and we can let our intuitions guide us. (Sometimes people do need a gentle "kick in the pants" when their grieving goes on and on.)

3. Learn to embrace our experiences with grief. We can see them as opportunities to grow.

4. Develop more gentle acceptance and appreciation of the aging process in our own lives.

5. Find ways to be proactive about death and grief: Have the courage to speak and share emotions around these issues when they come up naturally – openly, with love and gentleness.

6. Start the conversation around death and dying with our loved ones sooner rather than later, letting intuition and courage be our guide.

7. Make end-of-life and funeral plans and share them with our loved ones. Visit sites like agingwithdignity.org and the Five Wishes Document, or my website, **www.changewithcourage.com**. Explore aging, death, and the afterlife and ponder the unknown future and the mystery of it all. If your parents aren't planning for the inevitable, start planning yourself and share your plans with your parents. Then, they can be gently and naturally guided to explore something that's difficult for them to approach.

8. In whatever creative ways that we can, help hospitals to create a more gentle, loving space for death. This is beginning to happen, thanks to Palliative Care programs in numerous hospitals.

9. Get acquainted with local palliative care and hospice programs in your community; they are the way-showers for us in this area and can teach us a lot. Consider becoming a volunteer at a local hospice.

10. Become more knowledgeable about the death and grief rituals of our cultural and religious heritages. Then, broaden our horizons and become more knowledgeable about the rituals of other cultures and religions that are different from our own. They will have something to teach us.

20 Questions You've Always Wanted to Ask a Hospice Counselor

1. What is a good way to start the conversation with a family that has been avoiding the topic of death?

As a hospice counselor, I am often asked to be the bridge person between the family and the topic of death. Even when a member of the family comes onto hospice, many families have simply avoided bringing up the topic of what is really going on – a member of their family is coming very close to the end of their life. When I come onto the scene as a spiritual counselor, one of the things I need to facilitate, if at all possible, is to help the family talk about what's really going on, especially if the topic of death has not been broached. One of things that I enjoy doing is to use creative questions to help open the door to a topic that's been avoided.

Here are examples of some creative questions I have used, and that you might use with your friends and family members:

✦ Have you ever wondered about where we go after life here on earth ends? (What do you think it might be like in heaven?)

✦ Do you ever wonder what it might be like to see your Uncle Joe/your sister/your beloved one _____ again?

✦ Have you ever had a near death experience? (or a really powerful, vivid dream?) Have you ever had a mystical experience that left you pondering the Great Mystery? Have you witnessed a miracle that you could not explain?

✦ Have you ever wondered how the dream world connects to the afterlife?

✦ Are you able to recall your dreams? If so, have you ever received guidance or a prophetic (intuitive) "sense" about something going on in your life?

✦ What was your experience like around _____'s death? (when your loved one died)

✦ What brings you meaning in life? Is there something special (a gift) that your illness/disease is bring you at this time in your life? Or has brought you recently?

✦ What do you still wish to accomplish while you are alive? Are you writing these things down? Can you visualize them happening? Who could you ask for help (if you need to) to accomplish them?

✦ Whom do you still need to talk with (thank/forgive/say goodbye) before you die?

2. Don't you find your work depressing? How do you keep going, day after day?

Actually, hospice work for me has been some of the most life-giving, meaningful work that I've ever done. My guess is that the reason for this is at least two-fold: For one, whenever I have a conversation with someone on hospice (or their family member), we don't waste much time. We usually go into a deep and profound place very quickly; and I very much enjoy having those meaningful, heart-felt conversations with people. We may chitchat for awhile, but I'm the one who has the permission to probe deeper if I need to, and people are usually receptive to that because they realize they don't have lots of time to waste.

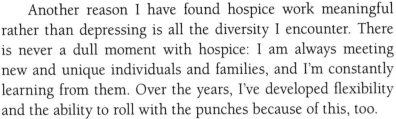

Another reason I have found hospice work meaningful rather than depressing is all the diversity I encounter. There is never a dull moment with hospice: I am always meeting new and unique individuals and families, and I'm constantly learning from them. Over the years, I've developed flexibility and the ability to roll with the punches because of this, too.

As I look back over the years that I have worked for hospice, it has been rather like having a kind of gradual near death experience. All that I learned and heard about death and grief had a way of expanding my theology and view of life. Speaking with people who were so close to the experience of death and grief, and hearing some very mystical stories and experiences – not to mention experiencing some of my own – gave me a sense of what it was like to be there myself; and my life was forever enriched and transformed because of it.

If any of you out there are interested in learning more about yourself and would like to deepen your understanding of the Universe and the mystery of life and death, I highly recommend that you look into becoming a volunteer with your local hospice. This would be a wonderful way for you to contribute to your community and to give yourself a huge gift in return!

3. How do you comfort someone in deep grief? Are there any good words to say to them?

Simply being with a person in deep grief can be very helpful. Be attentive and listen deeply to them with an open heart. Reach out to them with love, as their tendency will be to hibernate (hide in their own cave).

4. How do you talk with people who don't believe in God – or in an afterlife?

I remain open and allow them to have their point of view.

As the opportunity arises, I do suggest that they remain open to the possibility that there may be more than meets the eye in this world.

5. How can I best approach a person who's angry at God because of their circumstances?

At first I listen to them and hear them out. Usually a person who's angry at God is feeling victimized on some deep level; and they probably have good reason to feel this way. As I listen to them fully and attentively, their anger at God tends to soften. In this way, we often can get to a deeper place emotionally and begin to unravel what's really going on in their spiritual life and relationship with God.

6. What is the best way to talk with children about death?

Do it naturally and in a positive way; use any opportunity that comes along that you intuitively know is the right time and place to share. Children are so open spiritually that sometimes they can be our teachers in this area. Be open to whatever they might say in response to what you say; and be open to learn from them. They are much closer to Spirit than we adults are, so you may be surprised that they'll be able to see things that you cannot. (i.e., the story about the 17-mo.-old who waived bye-bye to grandpa – who had just died – in the family bed, mentioned in my first book, *The Last Adventure of Life.*)

7. As a hospice worker, how do you take care of yourself when you are grieving?

First, this is not always easy. I find that I can cry much more easily if I am grieving about something myself. Usually, I allow the tears to flow, as this can be a way of "giving permission" to those I'm with for their tears to flow, too. But when I am in deep grief, I must make sure that I'm taking care of myself properly. I may need to take a "mental health day" away from work, or

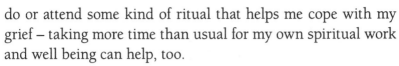

do or attend some kind of ritual that helps me cope with my grief – taking more time than usual for my own spiritual work and well being can help, too.

8. What enlivens you the most about your work? What is most challenging?

What enlivens me: The depth of sharing in conversation that I engage people in, the variety of people I am honored to meet and talk with, and the fact that I get to plant seeds and new ideas in people's minds.

What is most challenging: Sometimes, working within a rigid system that has its own agenda, and dealing with people and families who take the role of the victim.

9. How do you talk with a person or family who has a very different belief system or outlook on life than you?

Mostly, I wait for them to lead the way. I listen to what they share while withholding judgment. Chances are I have something to learn in these situations.

10. What is the difference between a bereavement counselor and a spiritual counselor?

Often, these two dovetail, as there is a piece of grief to be dealt with in most counseling. So one way to think about it might be that bereavement comes under the umbrella of spiritual counseling, which is much broader and in the context of hospice has more to do with helping people find what brings meaning to their lives when unexpected change occurs.

11. What is the most important thing to keep in mind when caring for a person close to death?

To honor them, who they are, their desires and needs; let them be in control as much as possible. Listen attentively to them; they are likely to give you helpful cues.

12. How can I be with someone who is getting ready to die? Will they even be able to hear me?

Probably the most important thing you can do for someone who is getting ready to die is to simply BE with them, in a gentle, caring, quiet way. Watch for the subtle cues that they will give you, for they will probably let you know in their own way what they would like.

Usually a person close to death has one foot in this world and the other foot in the next world. So, they will not be very focused or strong (grounded) in their being here on earth. You will need to honor their privacy and the fact that they are not "all here." It is best to let them guide the way. Even if they cannot speak with you, they may wish to hold your hand or have you close by. They may be able to squeeze your hand to give you a "yes" or some kind of sign that they agree with you, etc.

And yes, they will most definitely be able to hear you. If you doubt this, you might ask them to squeeze your hand if they can hear you. In the Tibetan Buddhist view, the soul can continue to hear for forty-nine days *after* the death has occurred. In that tradition a priest or someone from the temple comes to read to the soul of the dead person for at least forty-nine days after the death has taken place.

I sometimes have the opportunity to share with people who have recently lost their loved ones. Some have shared with me that they have wished they had not had their loved one's body whisked away after their death. Please keep in mind that you can take plenty of time with your loved one after they die. It is typical for the staff from the funeral home to come soon after the death to pick up the body, but you can ask them to come some hours (or in some cases even a day or two) later. Please ask for what you and your family need at this time.

I have also heard of people who regret not being there when their loved one passes. This is understandable, but the

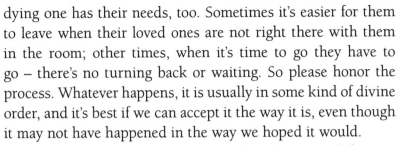

dying one has their needs, too. Sometimes it's easier for them to leave when their loved ones are not right there with them in the room; other times, when it's time to go they have to go – there's no turning back or waiting. So please honor the process. Whatever happens, it is usually in some kind of divine order, and it's best if we can accept it the way it is, even though it may not have happened in the way we hoped it would.

By the way, a couple of books besides mine (*The Last Adventure of Life* – Bridge to Dreams Publishing, 2005) that I recommend that people read around the very end of life are *Final Gifts* (Poseidon Press, 1992) and *Embraced by the Light* (Gold Leaf Press, 1992). These are both exquisite books that share courage and hope for those families faced with a loved one who is getting ready to die.

13. Are you often with a person who's dying? What is it like?

Interestingly enough, I find that I am rarely with a person when they die. Usually, by the time the death occurs on hospice, the family is comfortable enough with the process that they do not expect or require a spiritual counselor, chaplain, or even a hospice nurse to be with them. Sometimes the family does request a nurse to come out and verify that the death has occurred.

When I am at the bedside when a death is happening, it is usually a very sacred experience, not unlike a birthing experience. There's a sense in which being present takes your breath away. Sometimes you can almost feel another "presence" in the room.

Something to keep in mind is that no one can predict exactly when and how someone will die. Typically it is a very gradual, gentle process. The person's breathing slows way down and eventually just stops. I think of the quote from my book: "And dying you will leave your body as effortlessly as a sigh." (Psalm 121:8, Stephen Mitchell's translation) Another favorite quote along these lines is: "Death is absolutely safe! Like taking off a tight shoe . . ." (Emmanuel)

If you would like to read an account of a profound death I was blessed to be a part of through the use of some essential oils, I invite you to read pp. 41-43 in this book. This piece will help you see how beautiful death can be, even when there's been some degree of suffering (and stress) prior to it. The true key to the dying process, as with all change, is to relax. If you can relax, you can get through anything, even the biggest change we go through in life, the final transition.

14. What's the most important thing you have learned from doing hospice work?

I have learned and been gifted with so much: First of all, my theology has expanded so – like having had a near death experience myself. Secondly, my intuition, my ability to be more flexible in life, and my awareness of the interconnectedness of all have all developed in a strong way since doing hospice work. If you haven't already, you'll find these gleanings and much more shared throughout my reflections in this work.

15. Have you encountered mystical experiences on hospice? If so, how have they affected you?

Yes, by all means. I have had my own mystical experiences; I have also heard from many people about their mystical experiences. These have helped me see that there is so much more than meets the eye!

16. What is the most profound experience you've had doing hospice work?

Witnessing a very swift death of a man who was struggling with his breathing was probably the most profound experience I've had. I brought and anointed this man with essential oils,

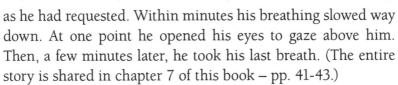

as he had requested. Within minutes his breathing slowed way down. At one point he opened his eyes to gaze above him. Then, a few minutes later, he took his last breath. (The entire story is shared in chapter 7 of this book – pp. 41-43.)

17. What, in your opinion, would help Americans better understand death?

I believe that Americans would be better off if they were more open and available to work with the inner life. Things like prayer, meditation, yoga, Qigong, and paying attention to one's dream world could make a big difference in people's lives – and their becoming more comfortable with death and the dying process.

18. What are some death and grief rituals that you have learned about that could assist us as we cope with these times in our lives?

This is a Japanese (Buddhist) custom: During the first year after a death, each day of the month that the person died – like the 5th, or 10th, for example – a priest or someone from the temple comes to pray and chant in the family home. This feels like a beautiful way to honor the grief that a family is experiencing.

Allowing people to have more time to be with the body after the death has occurred also seems like a very helpful custom. The Native American culture, for example, honors the three days before and after a person dies. These days are considered sacred, and one is encouraged to honor them with quiet reverence.

19. What is the best way to help someone in deep grief?

One of the best ways to communicate with a person in deep grief is to simply be with them. They may want to talk, or they may simply appreciate your reaching out to them. They may crave company, someone to just hang out with. Don't underestimate the power of simply being with someone in grief – a hug or a touch may mean more than words can say.

Some of the worst things a person can say after a friend or acquaintance loses a loved one are: Assumptions such as "I know what you're going through," "You'll get over it," or "God never gives a person more than they can handle." Often, unintentionally of course, we tend to say things that make *us* feel better. We want to fix the situation, whereas the person in grief needs comfort, consolation, and a listening ear. The grieving person usually craves simple "presence," a feeling that they can be held, cared for, and allowed to "be" exactly where and who they are in that moment.

Some of the best things we can say when a loved one is grieving are "I'm so sorry," "I love you (and your loved one who died)," or "I'm very sorry that you're having to go through this situation. Is there any way that I can help?" Sometimes silence is the best. You might simply give the grieving person a big bear hug and let them cry as much as they need. Then, you could let them know how much they're loved and that you will stand with them through this challenging time in whatever way they need. Intuition goes a long way here; gently let the grieving person guide the way, as everyone grieves differently.

A grieving person also needs to process what happened. Open-ended questions about what and how things happened are good, once they seem ready to talk. Questions like "What happened?" "How did your loved one die?" "How are you taking this all in?" "Tell me about how you're managing to cope with your loss?" can be helpful at this time.

Please don't hesitate to reach out to a grieving person. It means a lot to them; perhaps more than you'll ever know.

20. What would you like most to share with your readers? What is your most urgent, compelling message?

My deep hope and yearning is that people around the world, and Americans in particular, will come to be less afraid of death. As Rabbi Zalman Schachter-Shalomi has said, we have become awkward about dealing with death in the last 100 years by taking death to the hospital. It is imperative that we create more positive, gentle space for death in our hospitals and in our culture at large. And there is no reason that we cannot do this. We simply need to hold and create a new vision for death. We need to speak more openly about it in a pro-active way – before it is happening to us!

In Buddhist thought, the day you die is considered the most important day of your life. The moment of your death is the culmination of your entire life; and you want to be at the highest vibration possible in that moment so that you can move on to the highest vibration possible on the Other Side. (For more on the Buddhist perspective on death, I highly recommend that you read *The Tibetan Book of Living and Dying*, in particular Chapter 14, pp. 223-243. Chapters 13 and 15 are also very helpful.)

Crazy Horse, a holy man of the Lakota people, became well known for the phrase "Today is a good day to die." His words epitomized the Native American philosophy that understands that our lives are cyclical. Life on mother earth is a circle just as the stars; the moon and the sun are circles. We are born, we live, and we die. Crazy Horse and the holy men and women of the many tribes of what is now North and South America were indeed great prophets.

It is my fervent hope that this book will help you get ready for your death. You will learn about some of the best kept secrets of hospice. You will learn how expansive your life is and how lovingly, creatively, and graciously you might live it.

And who knows? You just might decide – as the Celtic way suggests – to die before you die, so that when you finally let go of your earthly life, there'll be no need to die.

Suggested Bibliography

Anam Aire, Phyllida. *A Celtic Book of Dying: Watching with the Dying, Traveling with the Dead*. Scotland, UK: Findhorn Press, 2005.

Bushnell, O.A. *Molokai*. Honolulu, HI: World Publishing Co., 1963.

Byock, Ira, M.D. *Dying Well: The Prospect for Growth at the End of Life*. New York: Riverhead Books, 1997.

Callanan, Maggie and Patricia Kelley. *Final Gifts: Understanding the Special Awareness, Needs, and Communications of the Dying*. New York: Poseidon Press, 1992.

Casarett, David J., M.D., *Last Acts: Discovering Possibility and Opportunity at the End of Life*. New York, NY: Simon & Schuster, 2010

Eadie, Betty Jean. *Embraced by the Light*. Placerville, CA: Gold Leaf Press, 1992.

Childs Gowell, Elaine, A.R.N.P, Ph.D. *Good Grief Rituals: Tools for Healing: A Healing Companion*. Barrytown, NY: Stanton Hill Press, 1992.

Dancing Heart, Maria. *The Last Adventure of Life: Sacred Resources for Living and Dying from a Hospice Counselor*. Findhorn, Scotland: Findhorn Press (2nd edition), 2008.

Gilbert, Elizabeth. *Eat, Pray, Love*. New York, NY: Viking, The Penguin Group, Inc., 2006.

Goble, Diane, MSCC. *Beginner's Guide to Conscious Dying*. Sisters, OR: Cosmic Creativity, 2009.

Groves, Richard F. and Henriette Anne Klauser, Ph.D. *The American Book of Dying: Lessons in Healing Spiritual Pain*. Berkeley, CA: Celestial Arts, 2005.

de Hennezel, Marie. *How the Dying Teach Us How to Live*. Lancaster Place, London: Warner Books, 1998 (Alfred A. Knopf Inc., 1997).

Housden, Maria. *Hannah's Gift: Lessons from a Life Fully Lived*. New York: Bantam Books, 2002.

Kessler, David. *The Rights of the Dying: A Companion for Life's Final Moments*. New York: HarperCollins Publishing, Inc., 1997.

Kovacs, Betty J., Ph.D. *The Miracle of Death: There is Nothing but Life – To Experience This Essential Truth Is to Experience the Miracle of Death*. Claremont, CA: The Kamlak Center, 2003.

Kübler-Ross, Elisabeth, M.D. *On Death and Dying: What the Dying Have to Teach Doctors, Nurses, Clergy and Their Own Families*. New York: Macmillan Publishing Co., Inc., 1969.

Lawson, Lee. *Visitations from the Afterlife: True Stories of Love and Healing*. New York: Harper San Francisco, 2000.

Levine, Stephen. *Who Dies? An Investigation of Conscious Living and Conscious Dying*. New York: Anchor Books, Doubleday, 1982.

Morse, Melvin, M.D., with Paul Perry. *Closer to the Light: Learning from the Near-Death Experiences of Children*. New York: Villard Books, 1990.

Palmer, Greg. Death: *The Trip of a Lifetime*. HarperSanFrancisco, 1993.

Price, Jan. *The Other Side of Death*. New York: Ballantine Books, 1996.

Rinpoche, Sogyal. *The Tibetan Book of Living and Dying*. New York: HarperCollins Publishers, 1993.

West, John. *The Last Goodnights: assisting my parents with their suicides [A Memoir]*. Berkeley, CA: Counterpoint, 2009.

Wilber, Ken. *Grace and Grit: Spirituality and Healing in the Life and Death of Treya Killam Wilber*. Boston, MA: Shambhala Publications, Inc., 1993.

Index

About the Author

As far back as she can remember Rev. Maria Hoaglund has been living outside the box. Even when she spoke fluent Japanese and was a goody two shoes working at obeying all the rules in Japanese public schools (through 8th grade) – so she wouldn't stand out more than she already did – she could not fit in the box because she did not look Japanese.

Maria also has the distinction of being conceived in the U.S., and then born in Tokyo, Japan after her parents arrived to serve as Lutheran missionaries there. Bridge-building was in her blood from the get-go. Maria's parents had to spend their first two years in Japan studying the language; Maria hopes that she brought her parents a measure of happiness as a new little bundle of joy at that challenging time in their lives.

Rev. Maria Dancing Heart Hoaglund is an author, transformational healer, U.C.C. minister, and end-of-life coach. Her first book, *THE LAST ADVENTURE OF LIFE: Sacred Resources for Living and Dying from a Hospice Counselor* is a unique inspirational resource book that honors the oneness of all things. It is assisting people who desire to face the end-of-life – and all kinds of change – with courage and hope. Many spiritual traditions are represented here. Maria shares from her rich experience with hospice that has opened up her own spiritual life. Anyone facing death, grief, or a transition of some kind would find her book and resources helpful.

One of Maria's passions is the body-mind-spirit healing modalities. Maria has developed a line of gift baskets called "Soul Baskets," or Transformational Healing Bundles, incorporating some of the many body-mind-spirit tools for healing and relaxation from the last chapter of her first book.

Maria considers herself a bridge builder who encourages more joy and awareness around living and dying. Her books will help you bring death back to life! She also writes for Examiner.com as their National Transitions & Grief Examiner.

See her websites for more:
www.changewithcourage.com, www.soulbaskets.com,
and **http://tinyurl.com/msv6aw.lives**

Acknowledgements

First and foremost, I want to thank Spirit and my guides, friends, and angels on the Other Side for your patience, love, and support. I so appreciate your constant presence with me and your gentle prodding along the way. I also appreciate Mother Earth's constant love and beauty so very much. I am grateful to my many friends and colleagues who have walked with me through the journey of staying on task and encouraging me to write this book. In particular, I want to thank my dear friend Cathy Tinker for her gracious, steady, and loving support. Thanks to Steve Bianucci and John Petellat (who I met through my first book), Halley Hart, David Gehrig, Nan Waldie, Adele Donaldson, and all my colleagues at Group Health. Many thanks to my editors and encouragers, Barbara Fandrich and Edmond Nickson, and to Linda Wilson and the good folks at Snohomish Publishing.

I want to thank all those I have served over the years of my hospice work. You have each contributed to my learning and growth in your own unique way. Thank you for allowing me into your life at a most sacred and special time.

I also wish to thank my dear daughter, Heather, who has been a support and God-send in so many ways. Thanks for a wonderful website that gets updated regularly, not to mention your inspiration and good technical, computer, and web support. Thanks to all of you who have contributed financially and otherwise to my efforts. My gratitude in advance, too, to all you readers, for your ongoing support to help me get this work out into the world. Every bit of your support and "spreading the word" makes a difference.

Also, I am deeply grateful to Josephine Wall and her art work. I first came across her "Earth Angel" thanks to a dying man's wife who had a large rendition of it on the wall at the end of his bed. Ever since, it has been a symbol and inspiration for my work.

ORDER FORM

I would like to order additional copies of
The Most Important Day of Your Life:
Are You Ready?

Name: _____

Mailing Address: _____

_____

_____

Your email, so that author can reach you:

_____

Quantity _____ x $11.95 each = subtotal _____

Sales Tax 9.5% (WA Only): _____

Domestic Shipping & Handling ($4/book): _____
(FREE shipping for 3 or more books)

International Shipping & Handling
($12/book; Canada: $7/book): _____

Total Due: _____

Send Check or Money Order to:
Bridge to Dreams
13619 Mukilteo Spwy., D5-411
Lynnwood, WA 98087

For presentations, book signings, and/or
more information, please contact
Maria Dancing Heart via email at:
info@changewithcourage.com
www.changewithcourage.com

For Dancing Heart's unique Japanese-style Soul Bundles, see:
www.soulbaskets.com